# MR. MONKEY IN THE TREE

# MR. MONKEY IN THE TREE

## BY MERNA HARRINGTON

## WRITTEN FOR MY JAYLAH

**Cover Design by Merna Harrington**
**Editing by Merna Harrington**
**Photos by Pixabay.com**
**Copyright © 2015 by Merna Harrington**
**All rights reserved.**

**ISBN- 13: 978-0692549988**
**ISBN- 10: 0692549986**

**First Edition First Printing**

**This book is dedicated to
an amazing little girl,
I love you Little Miss!
To all of the wonderful children of the world,
You are spectacular!!!**

**Zoo**

Ages 1 - 7

**I SAW A MONKEY.**

**MR. MONKEY IN THE TREE.**

HE WAS SMILING AND WAVING BANANAS AT ME.

I ASKED MR. MONKEY, MR. MONKEY IN THE TREE. TELL ME, WHY ARE YOU WAVING BANANAS AT ME?

MR. MONKEY EXCLAIMED, WELL I WAS WAVING HELLO! I DIDN'T WANT YOU TO GET BORED AND GO. I LOVE WHEN BOYS AND GIRLS COME TO SEE ME AT THE ZOO! IF YOU DIDN'T COME TO SEE ME I'D BE SAD AND BLUE.

WHEN I SEE YOUR BRIGHT FACES AND YOU CALL OUT TO ME, MY HEART GETS SO HAPPY I HAVE TO COME OUT OF MY TREE!

WOULD YOU LIKE A BANANA? I HAVE ONE FOR YOU. AND I HOPE YOU'LL COME TO SEE ME AGAIN HERE AT THE ZOO.

THE END

NOW LET'S PLAY A GAME, TURN THE PAGE...

# WHAT DOES MR. MONKEY HAVE FOR YOU?
# HOW MANY ARE THERE?

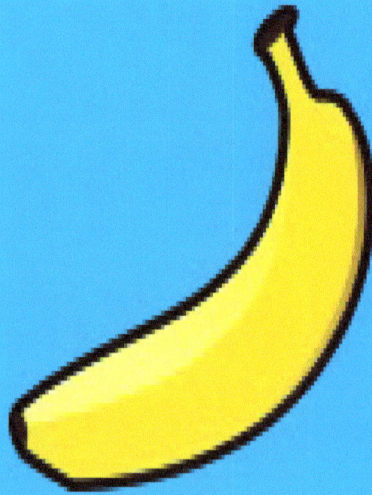

# NAME THESE INSECTS
# HOW MANY ARE THERE?

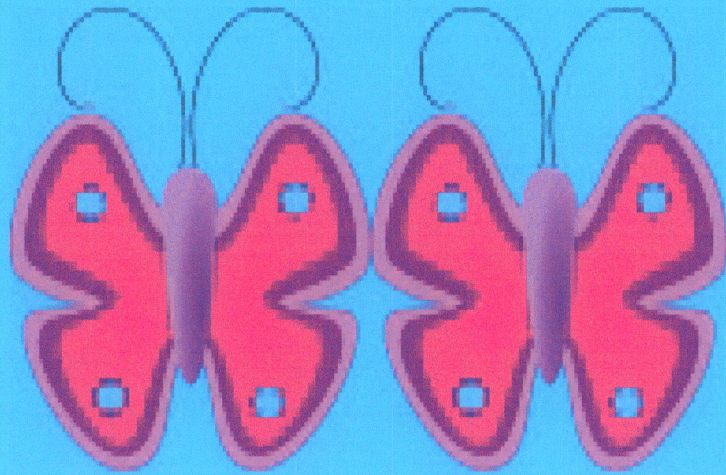

# WHAT ARE THESE?
# HOW MANY ARE THERE?

# NAME THE ANIMAL
# HOW MANY ARE THERE?

# NAME THE ANIMAL
# HOW MANY ARE THERE?

# NAME THE ANIMAL
# HOW MANY ARE THERE?

## ABOUT THE AUTHOR

MERNA HARRINGTON IS THE AUTHOR OF, "ABUSE IS NO ACCIDENT, IT'S DEFINITELY ON PURPOSE;" A BOOK WRITTEN TO ENCOURAGE ANYONE WHO MAY BE GOING THROUGH, OR HAVE GONE THROUGH DOMESTIC VIOLENCE. IN HER SPARE TIME, MERNA ENJOYS READING, WRITING, NATURE, ANIMALS, AND MAKING PEOPLE SMILE. SHE HOPES THAT YOU ENJOYED "MR. MONKEY IN THE TREE," AND WOULD LIKE FOR YOU TO KNOW THAT MORE CHILDREN'S BOOKS ARE ON THE WAY. THANK YOU!

EMAIL: MRMONKEY_2015@YAHOO.COM

# MR. MONKEY IN THE TREE

## BY MERNA HARRINGTON

COME ENJOY RHYME TIME HERE AT THE ZOO, MR. MONKEY WOULD LIKE TO SHARE SOMETHING WITH YOU! MR. MONKEY IN THE TREE MAKES READING AND COUNTING FUN FOR YOUR LITTLE ONES. HE TEACHES THE BEAUTY OF LOVE, KINDNESS, AND SHARING. CHILDREN WILL ENJOY SPENDING TIME WITH MR. MONKEY, AND YOU WILL TOO!